I SPEAK KIND

Published by Ali Gator Productions

First Published 2022

National Library of Australia Cataloguing–in-Publication (CIP) data:
Authors: Kareema Toutounji & Ahmed Teba, Illustrator: Sumaya Asvat, I Speak Kind Words
ISBN: 978-1-921772-81-8
For primary school age, Juvenile fiction, Dewey Number: 823.92

ALi GATOR

T: +61 (3) 9386 2771
P.O. Box 2536, Regent West, Melbourne Victoria, 3072 Australia
E: info@ali-gator.com W: www.ali-gator.com

This pretty cool
BOOK belongs to
a pretty cool **MUSLIM**
named:

____

____

____

Dedicated to our kids
who honoured us
when we became parents
and our parents
who honoured us
when we were kids.

I speak kind words
like my
Prophet (PBUH),
because he is
my perfect example.

PBUH - *Peace Be Upon Him*

Speak good or
remain silent,
what does that mean?

Well, when you're excited for dinner
but instead of chicken soup,
you get...

...BEANS!

You will want to **MOAN** and **GROAN**, like a frog with a flu.

But, instead you can look at
your bowl
and say

"CHICKAREE DOO!"

...(or thank you will do).

See words are important, because
your whole body can **HEAR!**
Your limbs hear everything you say,
that's, right! Not only your **EARS.**

When we say nice things,
your body will feel it through
and around.

From where your curls meet the

SKY.

To where your toes touch the

GROUND.

Speak nice to the

PLANTS.

Speak nice to the

ANTS.

SPEAK NICE TO THE WALLS

IT MAKES ALL THE DIFFERENCE

WHEN YOU HEAR A KIND WORD
AFTER A FALL.

And if you want to say something that isn't too kind...

remember there is always
a kind way to speak your mind.

Think of the words,

then PONDER

and

POUT.

Take a moment

BREATHE

before you let them out.

Because nice words from a loved one are like a hug full of

CHEER.

Tell your sister you love her and watch her smile from

EAR TO EAR.

So the next time you want to speak to yourself, **DADDY** or even an apple, remind yourself.

I speak kind words like my Prophet (PBUH), because he is my perfect example.

PBUH - *Peace Be Upon Him*

THERE'S ALWAYS A NICE WAY OF SAYING SOMETHING.

Let's have a chat about how we can say some kind words and follow our perfect example.

LET'S TRY

What is a different way to say **'GO AWAY'**?

What are some kind things you like **TO SAY** to others?

What are some kind things you like **TO HEAR** from others?

What is a different way to say **'I LOVE YOU'**?

What happens when we **SPEAK & HEAR** kind words?